A PARENT'S
LITTLE INSTRUCTION BOOK

D1584358

A PARENT'S
LITTLE INSTRUCTION BOOK

JASMINE BIRTLES

BOXTREE

First published in Great Britain in 1996 by
Boxtree Limited, Broadwall house, 21 Broadwall, London SE1 9PL.

Copyright © Jasmine Birtles

10 9 8 7 6 5 4 3 2

ISBN: 0 7522 2266 X

Cover design: Shoot That Tiger!
Page design: Nigel Davies

Printed and bound in the United Kingdom by Redwood Books, Trowbridge, Wiltshire.

A CIP catalogue entry for this book is available from the British Library.

FOREWORD

Do you have a happy family or are the kids still at home? Having a family means coping with tantrums, food thrown at the wall, potty training and worse - and that's just the father.

Children can be pretty messy too. This book is for long-suffering parents and frustrated offspring alike. It's for mums who have found out the hard way that childcare is learnt from the bottom up, and for dads who know that insanity is hereditary – you learn it from your kids.

What's the best form of contraception?
Kids.

• • •

Natural birth control:
showing your husband the contents of
your first child's nappy.

What do you call couples who use
the rhythm method? Parents.

• • •

Birth control is a way of
avoiding the issue.

The technical name for the father of twins:
Pas de deux.

• • •

An alarm clock is an object used
to wake up people who don't have children.

You know nothing about a man until
he's changed his first nappy.

• • •

If you're wondering what kind of child to have,
go for a grandchild.

Don't worry if you find
that you're
talking to yourself –
it's called being a parent.

Having a family is like
having a bath
– it starts off all right
but later on it's not so hot.

If you want to set
a good example to
your children,
lie about your past.

Learn to laugh at yourself,
after all your children do.

• • •

Not every family suffers from insanity
– some of them enjoy it.

There is nothing that
proves the theory of heredity
more definitively than producing
a beautiful child.

You know you're an ugly child
if your father looks pleased
when people say you look like
the milkman.

By the time a baby is born, most mothers
have had a bellyful.

• • •

Anyone with a baby knows that childcare
is learned from the bottom up.

Early to bed and early to rise – probably means
there's a baby in the house.

• • •

Baby boys are just like their fathers
– bald, sleepy and babbling.

There's nothing like
having a baby
to make you realise it's a
changing world.

18

Being a millionaire used to mean
extreme wealth.
Now it just means you can keep your children
in computer games.

Anyone who says they sleep like a baby
has never had one.

• • •

A baby is a small creature that
gets you down during the day and up at night.

All babies are subject to change
without notice.

• • •

A baby is a perfect example
of minority rule.

The basic rule of babycare:
keep one end full and the other end empty.

• • •

Never change a baby's nappy
in midstream.

Definition of a nanny:
Someone you employ to care for your children,
wash their clothes and entertain their father.

• • •

When the baby cries at night who gets up?
The whole street.

Feed your baby onions so that you can
find him in the dark.

• • •

If you're wondering why babies suck their
thumbs so much, try tasting baby food.

Parents of twins often live in a
two-bedlam house.

• • •

Never let your children bath themselves
– they'll leave a ring around the room.

Jam is a commodity found on bread,
children and door-handles.

• • •

Children,
the penalty for sex.

It's called a family tree because you get
all kinds of parasites living in it.

• • •

You know your kids are wild if the babysitter
arrives in combat gear.

Give your child a telling off
every day. You don't have
to have a reason
– he'll always think of one.

If you can't afford to feed
all the family, start a game
of hide and seek
just before dinner.

The first five years of
a child's life is a period
of rapid change. In this time
a parent can age twenty years.

No wonder toddlers are confused
– no sooner do they learn
how to talk than
they're told to be quiet.

The only things toddlers throw
and then pick up again are tantrums.

• • •

A child's favourite toy is always the one
that belongs to his playmate.

Rearing a small child is as easy as
nailing a poached egg to a tree.

• • •

Double your shopping bill.
Take a toddler in your trolley.

If you can see the writing on the wall,
you should take the
crayons away from the kids.

Remember that children who watch
TV all their waking hours
will go down in history…
and maths and English and Science

35

You can always spot a future bad driver
at the local recreation ground.
He's the one who won't leave
the roundabout.

Remember, sound travels slowly.
The things you tell your
children now won't finally reach them
until they're about forty.

Out of the mouths of babes… come things they
shouldn't have heard their parents say.

• • •

The police have over ten million fingerprints.
So does any house with more than one child.

A child's next favourite toy is the one
he can't find.

• • •

Children's birthday parties last
until someone's been sick.

Parents seldom make the
same mistake twice…
it's usually three or four times.

Definition of walking:
what parents always did as children to
get to school, further than anyone else,
through more snow, up more hills
and with more joy and gratitude.

Things you wish your toddlers would say:
  – I want to go to bed now.
  – No, I've got enough toys, thank you.
    – Don't worry, I'll pay.
    – Can I clear up now?
– Look, I'll go to school and get out of your way.

Small children are physically unable
to have a pee unless they
are in a car on the motorway
with no conveniences for fifty miles.

Little boys' shorts look so big on them
they should be called 'longs'.

• • •

Definition of a childish game:
one in which your child beats you.

Children will not willingly share anything
except your secrets and their germs.

• • •

If your children are perfect angels,
a joy to be with and always
pleased to see you, you're their grandparent.

At least children never puts you on hold.

• • •

Never choose a child as a flatmate.
They won't pay the rent and
they always drink your milk.

Spice up your child's parties
– serve vodka jellies and ice–cream.

• • •

You know your child's sophisticated if the party
entertainer is a stripogram.

The toys that would sell out if only someone
made them:

- a bouncing alarm clock
- a just-in-reach pan handle
- a socket you can get a finger into

– a cat-flap big enough to crawl out of
and onto the motorway
– a dog-tail that isn't pulled away
– sugar-coated scissors
– edible dog-poo
– easy-throw food

What's the most effective food-blender
on the market? A three-year-old.

• • •

How can you tell that a child has been
sent away to school?
The crayon marks stop at the dado rail.

The best children's party venue:
someone else's house.

• • •

There is only one thing worse than children
making a noise:
children making no noise at all.

51

There are three main stages of childhood:
1) learning to crawl,
2) learning to walk,
3) learning to ask for money.

You know you're in trouble when,
in dealing with your three-year-old,
you start to sound like
a three-year-old.

The first thing a boy learns
when he gets a drum is that he's never
going to get another one.

• • •

Make the most of taking a child out to eat –
send him round foraging for food.

If your child won't eat his food,
dress it up as mud.

• • •

Definition of first-time parents:
people who are anxious for their child
to start talking.

How to deal with a sticky child:
1) clean him up,
2) put him outside to be washed by the rain, or
3) hang him up and use him as flypaper.

If your child asks how Father Christmas
gets into the house just tell her
that he comes through a large hole
in daddy's wallet.

A child is a small, sweet thing
with mafia tendencies.

• • •

The best reason to have a child
is so that at least someone
will be able to programme the VCR.

To err is human.
To screw up is completely parental.

• • •

You know your child is unpopular
if even his imaginary friend
won't play with him.

Forget family loyalty,
when it comes to persuading a child
to do something, nothing is as effective
as bribery and corruption.

If he's not on drugs, mugging old ladies and
breaking into sweet shops you can
congratulate yourself on
producing a well-adjusted six-year-old.

A child's ideal disease is one that:
– gets him off school for three days
– only comes on at eight in the morning
– doesn't stop him watching telly
– is cured with chocolate and milkshakes.

Childhood laws of physics:
- You will only get hurt if there is a
  grown-up there to see it.
- Summer lasts five years.
- Snow is only fun until it gets into your mittens.
- Socks were meant to be in the bottom of
  wellingtons and not on your feet.

Children are like half-sucked sweets
– small, sticky and covered in fluff.

• • •

Every parent knows that
'Because I say so…' is the fundamental
answer to all known questions.

Never go out with a child who
is better dressed than you.

• • •

Every child in the world knows
that when his parents say
'This is the last straw' – it isn't.

Children like simple toys such as teddy bears,
dolls and video recorders.

• • •

Definition of family planning:
working out how to keep the
children occupied for the whole weekend.

Of all the animals a small boy is the most
unpredictable.

• • •

The best way to make children understand
the value of money is
to charge things to their credit cards.

They say that computers are so
user-friendly nowadays that even
a child can understand them.
Actually, only children can
understand them.

Handy hint:
if you want to get a lid
that's stuck off a jar,
leave it lying around the house and
tell the kids not to touch it.

Thank goodness children never try
to boost your ego.

• • •

Never ask a child its opinion of
your most fashionable item of clothing
– it will always be honest.

There is nothing like the joy of motherhood
– especially when they're asleep in bed.

• • •

It's very difficult to keep young,
these days, especially if you
have three or four of them.

Children should be seen and not had.

• • •

A jumper is an item of clothing
worn by your child when you feel cold.

If your parents didn't have any children
it's likely that you won't either.

• • •

A child is the hardest thing in the world to raise
– especially in the mornings.

Remember, it's never too late to have
a happy childhood.

• • •

Definition of the school run:
the thirty-second dash between your illegally
parked car to the school door and back again.

A modern home is one where a switch
can control everything but the children.

• • •

Parents who buy a set of drums
for their children either love them too much
or hate their neighbours more.

Try and have your children properly spaced
– about half a mile between each one.

• • •

If you want to attract your children's attention
just sit down and look comfortable.

Don't waste your neighbour's time
telling him how impressive
your children are, he wants to tell you
how impressive his are.

Never trust a child with his
hands behind his back.

• • •

Never trust a child with
sugar round his mouth.

With kids in the house,
cleanliness is next to impossible.

• • •

Remind your children to do unto others
before they do it to you.

Make sure you embarass your
children properly in their early years
because they will certainly
do it to you later on.

Encourage your children to
find sensible ways of earning
their pocket money
– stockbroking for example.

School is important to a child's development.
It gives them another place to run away from.

• • •

Tell your children that schooldays
are the best days of their lives
– unless you're a teacher.

Children brighten a home
– they never turn the lights off.

• • •

A babysitter is someone you pay by the hour
to eat all your food and let your kids
do what they want.

There are three types of lies:
lies, damned lies, and
what happened to the school report.

A boy and his bicycle
are seldom parted.

• • •

A harrassed mother has several mouths
to feed and one very big one that she listens to.

Setting a good example takes all the fun
out of adulthood.

• • •

If holidays really meant getting away
from it all, families would split up
and take separate trips.

Make your children clean
their own rooms,
that way you'll always have
somewhere in the house to eat.

Having a child in the house
just gives you something else to dust.

• • •

If you don't believe in the theory of relativity,
just try marrying someone with a large family.

Dinner time is when children join their parents
at the table and watch them eat.

• • •

If you want your children to learn to count,
give them different amounts of pocket money.

Teenagers believe in free speech – particularly in long-distance calls from your phone.

• • •

Families take their holidays to get away
from it all which is why they go to camps full of
screaming kids and angry parents.

You know your daughter has grown up
when she's all skin and phones.

• • •

Make sure your children don't get a police record.
It would stop them getting into parliament and
becoming proper criminals.

If you want to stop your teenagers reading porn magazines, make them required reading at school.

• • •

Avoid car sickness
– don't allow your children to drive it.

If your children want to learn to drive
don't stand in their way.

• • •

It used to be that growing up meant getting
all your questions answered. Now it means
you get all your answers questioned.

An education is what parents receive when
they sit in on a conversation between teenagers.

• • •

Definition of genetics: the study of
which parent's family is responsible for their
teenager's behaviour.

Never lend your car to anyone
with whom you share the bathroom.

• • •

Getting the baby to sleep is hardest
when he's about eighteen years old.

There's nothing wrong with teenagers
that reasoning won't aggravate.

• • •

Never try to amuse a teenager
– it breaks their concentration on boredom.

Teenagers with acne should decorate
their rooms in polka-dot wallpaper and blend in.

• • •

Teenagers are like vampires:
they shrink from the light and suck you dry.

If your teenage son hides copies of *Playboy*
under his bed it's normal.
If you can't find the bed for the piles
of magazines – he's a pervert.

Only teenagers understand why homework
is best done in front of the TV,
with headphones on while
they're playing computer games.

A teenager's idea of a balanced diet:
a hamburger in each hand.

• • •

Young teenagers' idea of a good snog:
getting their braces locked together.

The cleverest part of doing homework is
thinking up the excuse.

• • •

It rarely occurs to teenagers that
the day will come when they know as little
as their parents.

101

Parents of university students
get poorer by degrees.

• • •

You should be understanding with boys
while they are going through that awkward age
– between ten and forty.

If you want your teenage son to clear the garage,
tell him he can use the car.

• • •

Don't let your teenagers listen to too much
hard rock, they'll get metal fatigue.

God made bus stops
as nests for teenagers.

• • •

Why don't teenagers tell you
where they're going?
Because they don't know.

A teenager's natural habitat
is in your pocket.

• • •

The trouble with life's questions is that
when you're old enough to know the answers
you've forgotten the questions.

Teenagers live in a world of their own
– it's called Boredom.

• • •

On average a teenage girl spends ten minutes
a day with her best friend and forty minutes
discussing her on the phone.

Teenagers are also known as
Parent-agers.

• • •

Ask not for whom the bell tolls
– if there's a teenager in the house,
it'll be a phonecall for her.

Teenagers are always starting things
they can't finish – like phonecalls.

• • •

If you want to be mean, give your children
batteries for Christmas with a label saying
'toys not included'.

When teenagers start sowing their wild oats
parents should start threshing.

• • •

It's a good thing that teenagers
don't ask to be born
– most of us would turn them down.

Teenagers know everything
except how to pay for themselves.

• • •

There is nothing like arguing with teenagers
to realise that you're not young enough
to know everything.

Adolescence is the age at which a child
feels its parents should be taught the facts of life.

• • •

Adolescence is the time when your kids stop
asking where they came from and start refusing
to tell you where they're going.

Teenagers are alike
in many disrespects.

• • •

When your teenager comes of age
employ a surgeon to be on standby
– to remove him surgically from your wallet.

Teenagers are hormones
with hair.

• • •

What's the difference between a sports car
and a teenager? One is noisy, oddly-shaped
and expensive, the other's a sports car.

Teenagers suffer mood swings
from passion to fashion.

• • •

There are three things you can
guarantee about teenagers:
1) they're on the phone all day and
2) I'm bored of this…

Things you wish your teenagers would say:
- I want you to impart your wisdom
  and experience to me.
- I don't think black is a good colour on me.
- Is my music too loud?
- Let me pay my phone bill.
- That's far too late! I'll be back at nine.

Definition of adolescence
– the period between puberty and adultery.

• • •

Posh parents like their daughters to marry early
so that they don't have to wait too long
for the alimony cheques.

Fathers are to dancing
what Madonna is to celibacy.

• • •

If you want to get your own back
live long enough to be a burden
to your children.

117

Definition of a mother
– guilt-edged insecurity.

• • •

Euthanasia means never having
to tell your parents you're sorry.

You're only a child once.
After that you need another excuse.

• • •

Raising children is like playing golf
– you think you'll do better the next time round.

We are all God's children
by a previous marriage.

• • •

Definition of poverty: having enough money
to buy all the things you ever wanted to have
if only you hadn't got children.

Charity and bribery
begin at home.

● ● ●

Money may not be everything but it keeps you
in touch with your children.

Insanity is hereditary
– you get it from your children.

• • •

Mothers always have at least three things
on their mind – are you eating enough?
when are you getting married?
and what was the first thing again?

Should women have children over forty?
No, forty children is quite enough.

• • •

If a boy is a lad and he has a step-father,
is the boy a step-ladder?

123

Anyone who thinks a mother is her own boss
has never had children.

• • •

Having a vasectomy is
the kindest cut of all.

Parental influence is a thing you think you have
until you try to use it.

• • •

I'm a pauper.
Congratulations! Boy or girl?

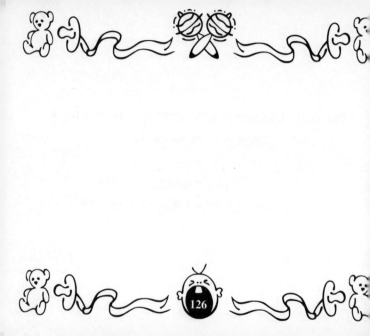

JASMINE BIRTLES

Jasmine is fully qualified to write about parenting as she herself has had parents and continues to enjoy ignoring them. She is also very much in touch with her inner child – so in touch in fact that she spoils it regularly with chocolate, crisps and trips to Disneyland. She loves to be around children of all ages – especially ones who can sign their names at the bottom of cheques – and hopes, one day, to persuade someone else to look after some of her own.